NAA P-51D-5-NA M

P-51D-5-NA. 1/72 scale plans.

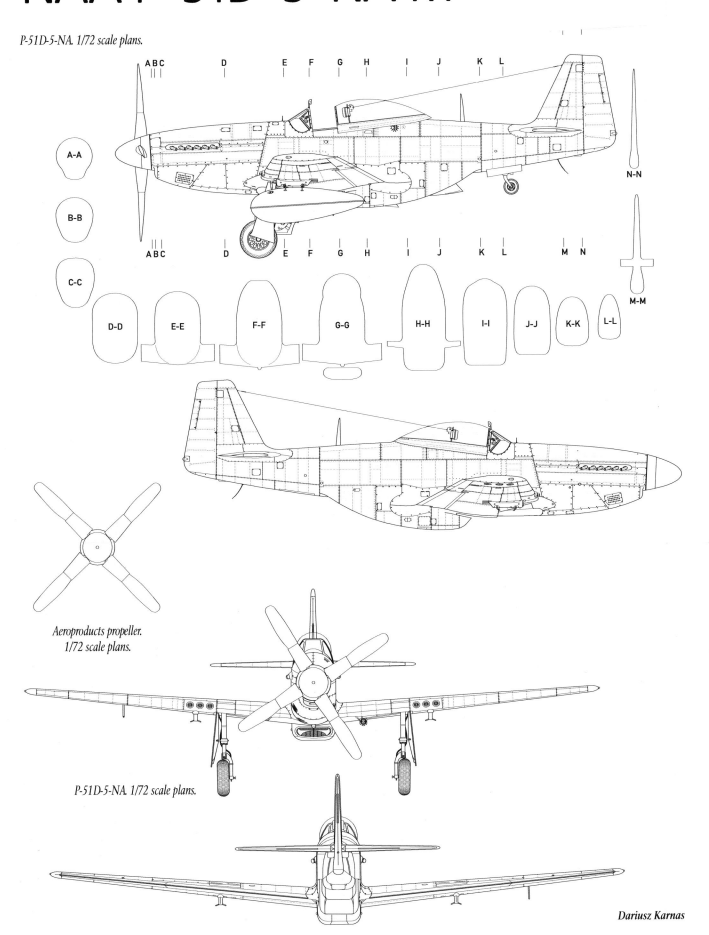

Aeroproducts propeller.
1/72 scale plans.

P-51D-5-NA. 1/72 scale plans.

Dariusz Karnas

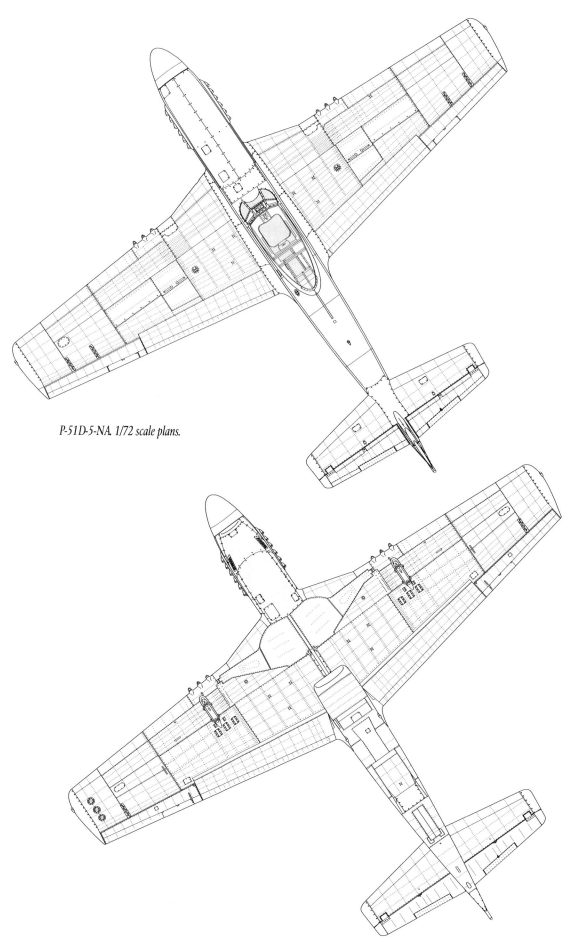

P-51D-5-NA. 1/72 scale plans.

Dariusz Karnas

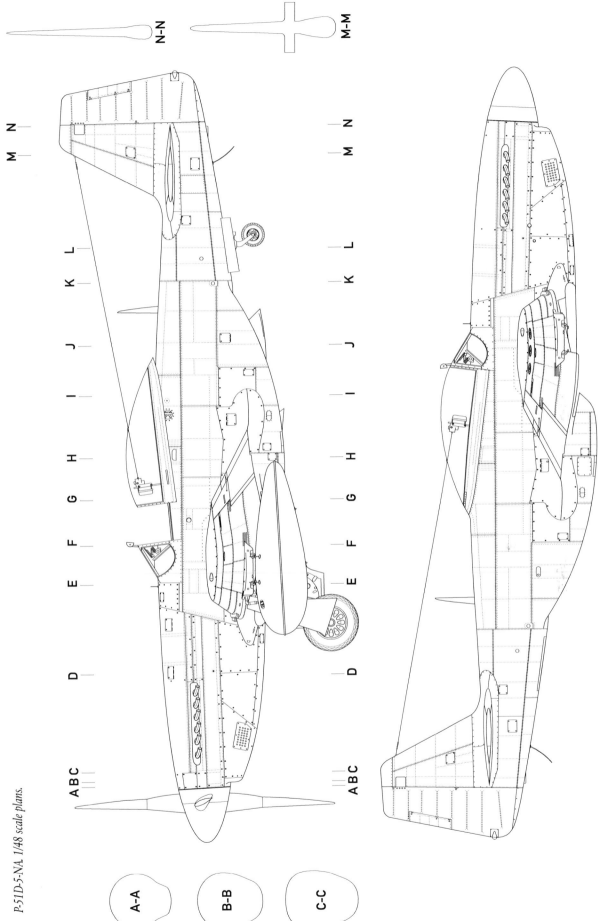

N-N

M-M

M N

M N

L

L

K

K

J

J

I

I

H

H

G

G

F

F

E

E

D

D

ABC

ABC

A-A

B-B

C-C

P-51D-5-NA 1/48 scale plans.

Dariusz Karnas

3

P-51D-5-NA. 1/48 scale plans.

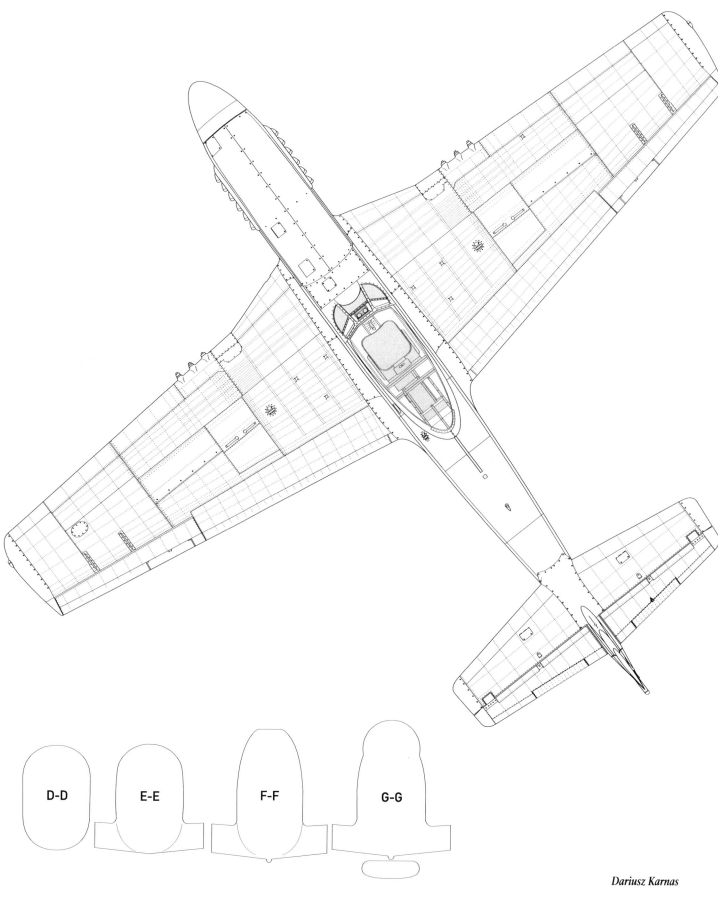

D-D E-E F-F G-G

Dariusz Karnas

P-51D-5-NA. 1/48 scale plans.

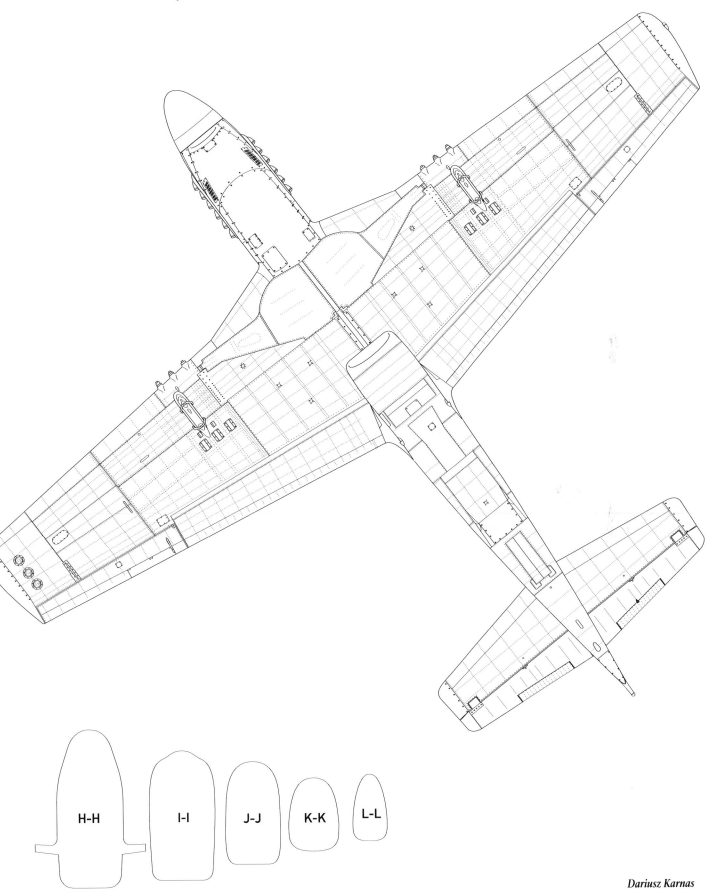

H-H   I-I   J-J   K-K   L-L

Dariusz Karnas

P-51D-5, 44-13366, in flight, without the dorsal fillet. (Mike Jerram via Roger Wallsgrove)

Mustangs of 361ˢᵗ FG in formation flight over England. Bubble top Mustangs are P-51D-5-NA version. E2-S has a retrofitted dorsal fillet. (USAF)

Two wartime photos of the early P-51D cockpit. (Mike Jerram via Roger Wallsgrove)

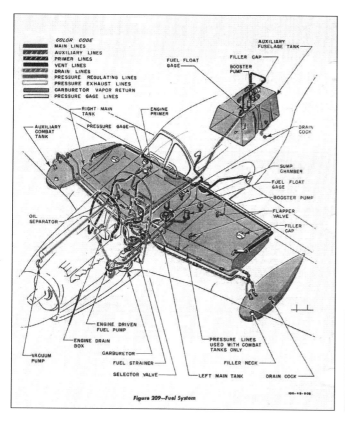

Fuel system. (Technical Manual)

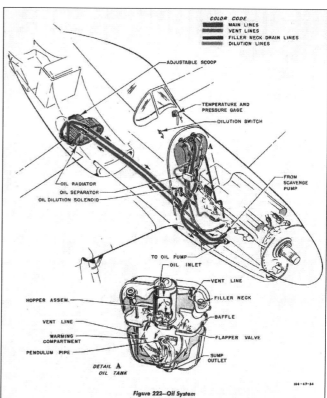

Oil system. (Technical Manual)

Cooling system. (Technical Manual)

Landing gear control system. (Technical Manual)

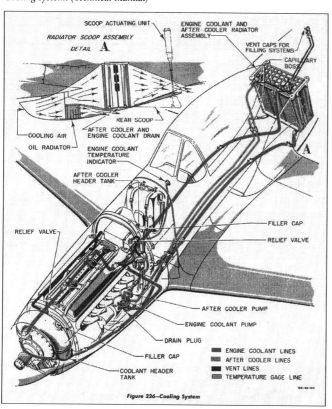

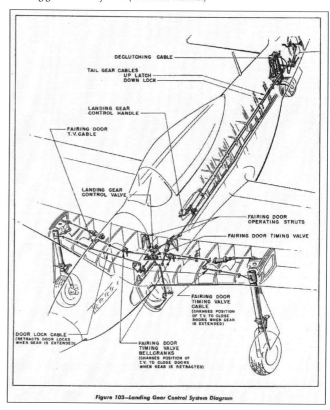

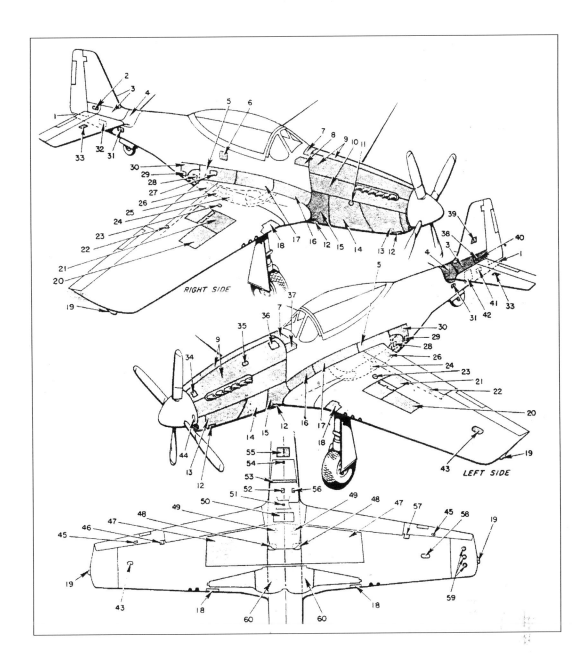

RIGHT SIDE

LEFT SIDE

Inspection and Access Panels.

1. Rudder Lower Hinge Access Fairing
2. Vertical Stabiliser Aft Right-hand Fairing
3. Vertical Stabiliser Forward Fairing
4. Fuselage to Horizontal Stabiliser Fairing
5. Aft Wing to Fuselage Fairing
6. Oxygen Filler Valve Access Door
7. Hydraulic Reservoir Access Cover
8. Oxygen Lines and Instruments
9. Engine Access Upper Cowlings
10. Engine Access Side Cowlings
11. Engine Crank Access Hole
12. Engine Heating Access Door
13. Engine Access Lower Forward Cowling
14. Engine Access Lower Intermediate Cowling
15. Engine Access Lower Aft Cowling
16. Wing to Fuselage Forward Fairing
17. Wing to Fuselage Intermediate Fairing
18. Main Landing Gear Pivot Shaft Access Door
19. Running Light Access
20. Ammunition Bay Access Door

21. Gun Bay Access Door
22. Aileron Cable Turnbuckle Inspection Cover
23. Wing Fuel Tank Filler Cap
24. Front Scoop Attachment Bolt Access
25. Oil Radiator Line Access Door
26. Aftercooler Line Hose Access
27. External Power Plug Access Cover
28. Radiator Cover Bolts Access Door
29. Radiator Cover Attachment Bolts Access Door
30. Radiator Cover Assembly
31. Tail Gear Down-lock Access Door
32. Tail Gear Up-latch Access Door
33. Elevator Trim Tab Actuating Drum Access Door
34. Coolant Tank Filler Neck Access Door
35. Aftercooler Tank Access Door
36. Oil Tank Filler Neck Access Door
37. Engine Controls and Instrument Access Cover
38. Rudder Trim Tab Cable Rollers Access Door
39. Rudder Trim Tab Actuating Cable Drum Access Door
40. Vertical Stabiliser Aft Left-hand Fairing
41. Rudder Bellcrank Access Door

42. Tail Gear Up-latch and Actuating Strut Access Door
43. Remote-reading Compass Access Door
44. Propeller Governor Access Door
45. Aileron Centre Hinge Access Door
46. Aileron Trim Tab Actuating Drum Access Door
47. Fuel Tank Doors
48. Fuel Booster Pump Access Doors
49. Fuel Tank Drain Cock Access
50. Oil Radiator Access Door
51. Oil Radiator Rear Scoop Actuating Rod Access Plate
52. Coolant Drain Access Door
53. Rear Scoop Hinge Access Door
54. Rear Scoop Actuating Rod Access Plate
55. Control Cable and Oxygen Cylinder Access Door
56. Aftercooler Drain Access Door
57. Aileron Boost Tab Actuating Fitting Door
58. Remote Contactor Mast Access Door
59. Recognition Lights and Access
60. Wheel Well Fairing Doors

9

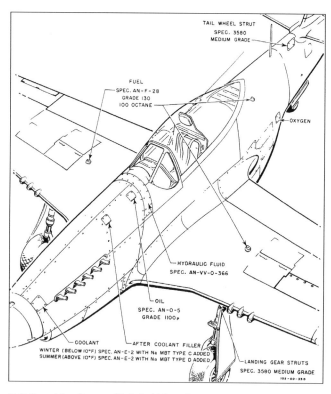

P-51D servicing diagram. (Technical Manual)

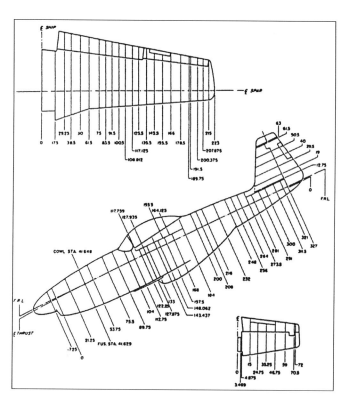

P-51 Stations Diagram. (Technical Manual)

Wing-fuselage fillet, note panel lines and access panels. (Dariusz Karnas)

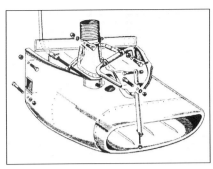

Above: *Drawing from Technical Manual showing radiator mounting system.*

Left: *A view of the radiator intake on VH-JUC. This is lower (further away from the fuselage) than the earliest Mustangs, and contains the oil and engine radiators, the oil cooler being below. (James Kightly)*

Below: *Main fuel tank filler cap and "Ground Here" jack. (Stratus)*

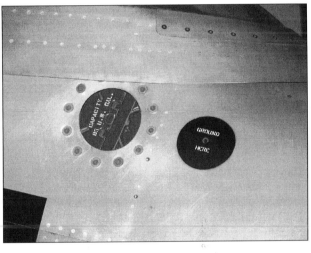

The radiator outlet with flap in the open position on the RAF Museum's Mustang. (Stratus)

Looking up and into the rear fuselage from the radiator position, of "Happy Jack's Go Buggy" showing the oxygen tanks and data case, all in the correct colours and details. Note also the control cables and their markings and tags shown. (Midwest Aero Restorations)

Starboard side of the radiator, all panel lines are clearly visible. (Stratus)

11

Above: Beautiful shot of the P-51D underside showing wing and fuselage details and partial D-Day markings. Note the lower image shows outlined D-Day stripes that are also at a different angle over the flaps. (US National Archives)

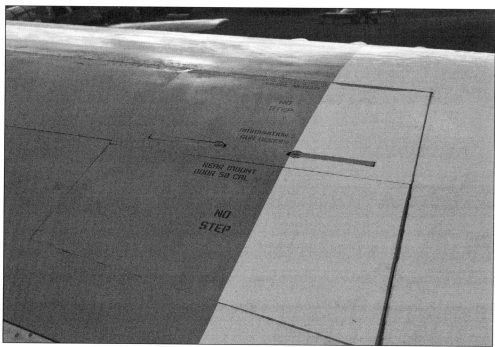

Right: Machine guns covers and latches. (Dariusz Karnas)

Two examples of the recognition lights on the underside of the starboard wing. Seen on the RAF Museum's Mustangs at Cosford and Hendon.

Details of of the starboard aileron and landing flap. (All Stratus)

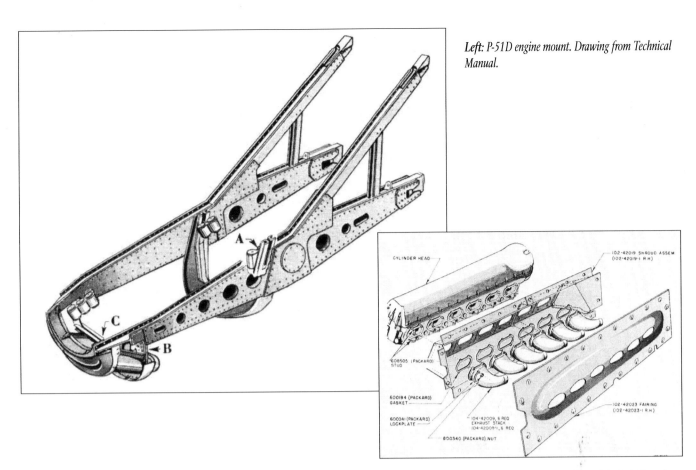

Left: P-51D engine mount. Drawing from Technical Manual.

Above: Details of the exhaust. Drawing from Technical Manual.

Left: Cowling supports.
Drawing from Technical Manual.

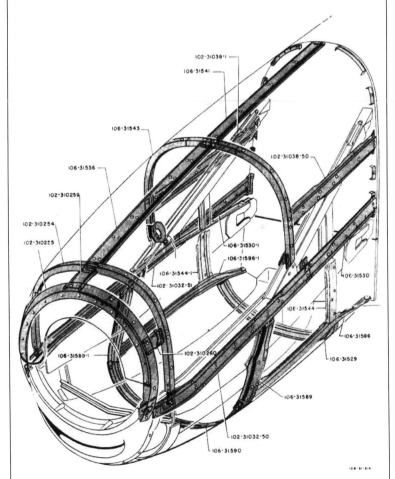

Early version of the pilot's seat. (P-51D Spare Parts Catalogue)

Opposite page top: *Adjusting the Magneto timing. All panels are removed. (Mike Jerram via Roger Wallsgrove).*

Opposite page bottom: *Australian used Packard Merlin engines built up as units to the Mustang production at Fisherman's Bend, Melbourne. It is rare to see the Mustang engine unit as a single separate item. (CAC via James Kightly)*

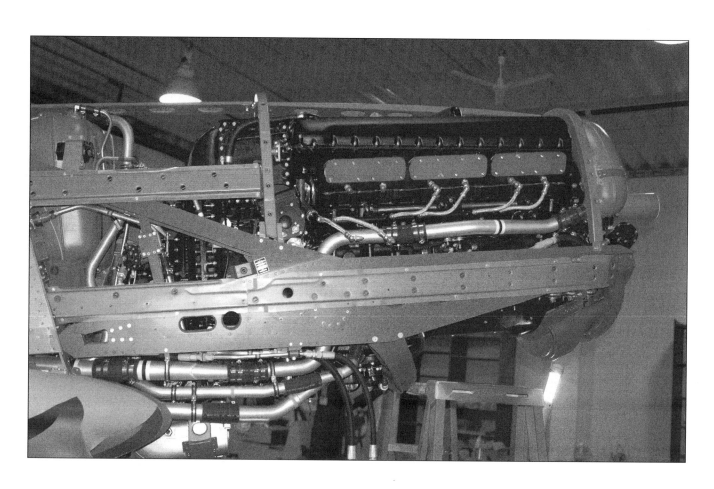

Opposite page top: The starboard side of the engine on "Happy Jack's Go Buggy" during installation. Note the different colours on the mounts, and the blanking plates on the cylinder-head before the exhaust stubs are fitted. These would have been similarly blanked off on newly supplied engines in wartime as well.
(James P Church)

Opposite page bottom: Complete V-1650-7 engine in situ. (Mike Jerram via Roger Wallsgrove)

Bottom: P-51D engine check before test flight. (Mike Jerram via Roger Wallsgrove)

Engine cowling and supports. Drawing from Technical Manual.

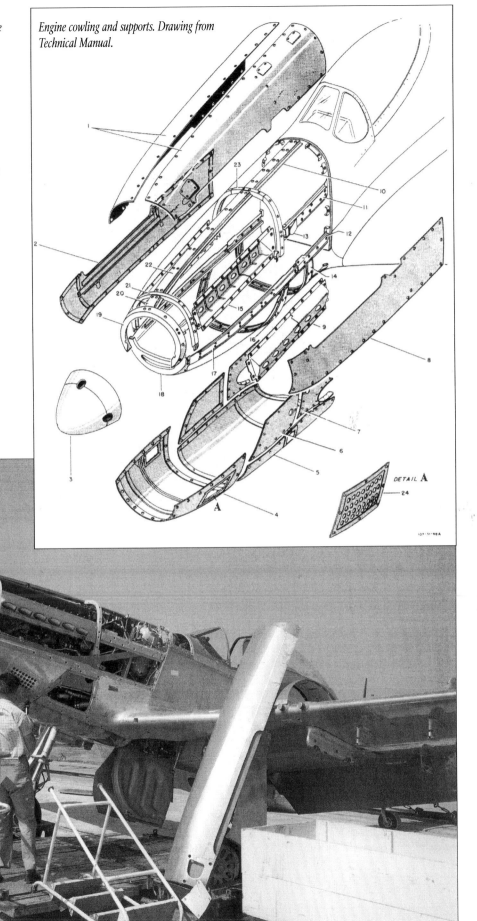

Above: Front view of the windscreen.
Below: Rear view of the canopy. Internal frame is visible.
(Both Stratus)

P-51D-5-NA, s/n 44-13641, WD-A of 335th FS, 4th FG, 8th AF. Aircraft was lost on 22 July 1944 with Lt. Lloyd G Kingham killed. (US National Archives)

P-51D-5-NA, s/n 44-13704, B7-H "Ferocious Frankie" of 374th FS 361st FG, July 1944. (US National Archives)

52nd Fighter Group, 4th Fighter Squadron aircraft:
P-51D-5-NA, s/n 44-13287, WD-M, "Miss Ruth" (stbd) & "Pendaja" (port) personal aircraft of Lt. William Parent;
P-51D-5-NA, s/n 44-13289, WD-X;
P-51D-5-NA s/n 44-13263, WD-D, "Jo-Baby" personal aircraft of Lt. Robert McCambell;
P-51D-5-NA, s/n 44-13485, WD-H, "Miss Rogers" personal aircraft of 1st Lt. James Daniel Callahan (only rudder is visible).
(US National Archives)

P-51D-5-NA, s/n 44-13357, "Tika IV", B7-R of the 374th FS, 361st FG, 8th AF. Aircraft assigned to Lt. Vernon R Richards. (US National Archives)

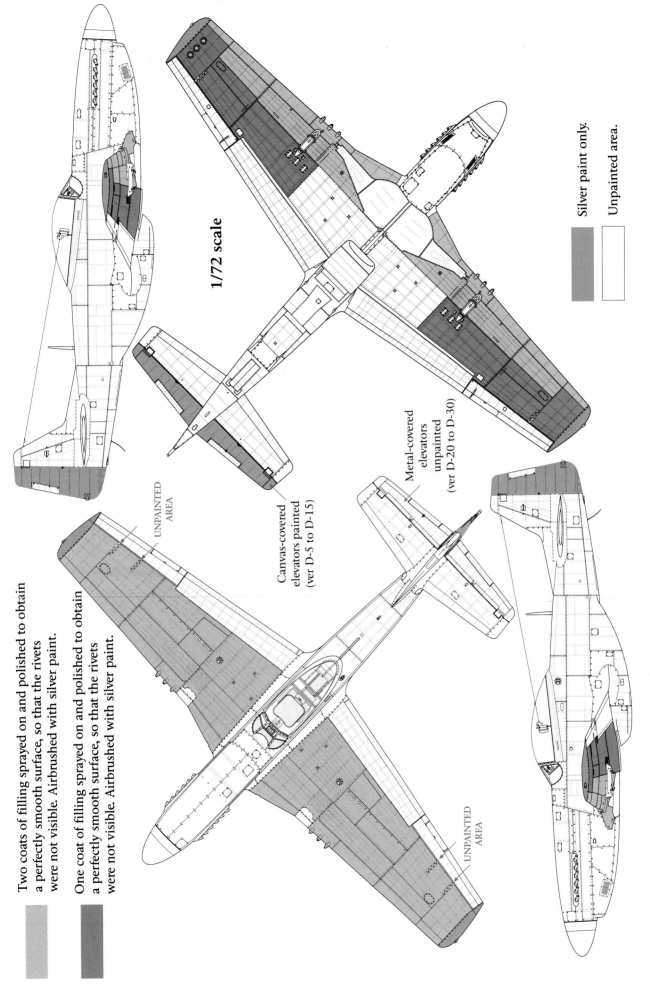

1/72 scale

Dariusz Karnas

Silver paint only.

Unpainted area.

Canvas-covered
elevators painted
(ver D-5 to D-15)

Metal-covered
elevators
unpainted
(ver D-20 to D-30)

UNPAINTED
AREA

UNPAINTED
AREA

Two coats of filling sprayed on and polished to obtain
a perfectly smooth surface, so that the rivets
were not visible. Airbrushed with silver paint.

One coat of filling sprayed on and polished to obtain
a perfectly smooth surface, so that the rivets
were not visible. Airbrushed with silver paint.

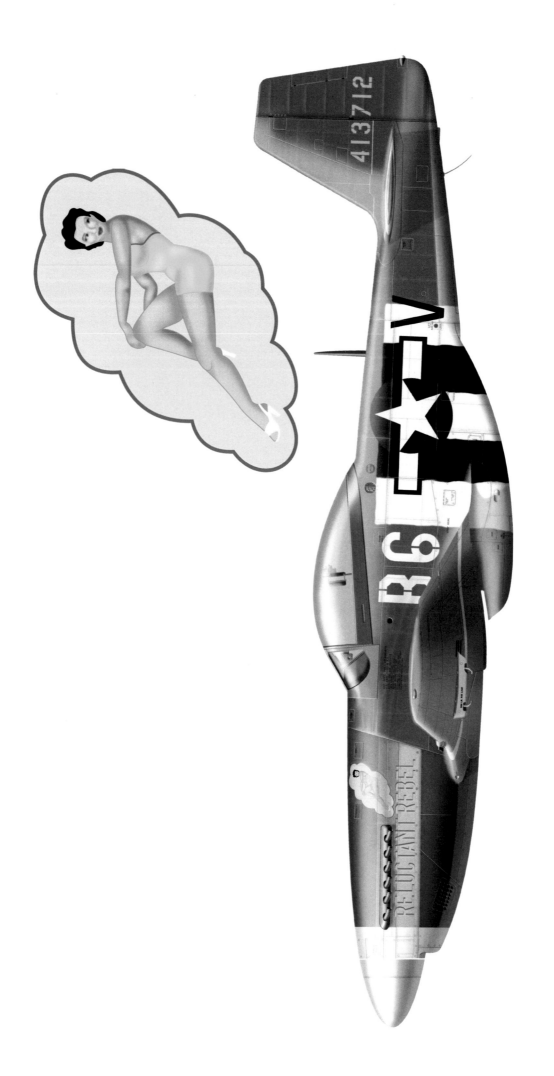

P-51D-5-NA Mustang, s/n 44-13712, B6•V, 363rd FS, 357th FG, 8th AF. July 1944. Maj. Robert W. Foy. Dark Green upper surfaces and Medium Sea Grey under surfaces, black and white invasion markings, white strips on wings and horizontal tail.

Artur Juszczak

P-51D-5-NA Mustang, s/n 44-13712, B6•V, 363rd FS, 357th FG, 8th AF. July 1944. Maj. Robert W. Foy.

Artur Juszczak

P-51D-5-NA Mustang, s/n 44-13712, B6•V, 363rd FS, 357th FG, 8th AF. July 1944. Maj. Robert W. Foy.

Artur Juszczak